Fish that Fool

Contents

Fish eat fish   2

Blending in   4

On the hunt   8

Going to ground   14

Fish that fool   22

Written by Inbali Iserles

Collins

Fish eat fish

It's hard being a fish. Hunters lurk in rivers and seas.

2

But fish have clever ways to avoid being eaten.

Blending in

This trout blends in with the creek.

A trout has patterns that **mimic** its **habitat**.

The green and brown patterns help trout
stay hidden in green riverbeds and streams.
But what if a fish's habitat is full of reds
and blues?

Frogfish lie on the reef near the beach.
The reef can be red, pink or blue.

Fish facts

Frogfish can shift how they look to blend in!

7

On the hunt

Blending in can help a fish **scout** for food.

Fish facts

Trumpetfish look like
floating driftwood.
They sway near little fish.
Then they attack!

Moray eels do not **pursue** meals. They blend in with the reef ...

Then they leap out to grab squid!

Fish facts

Moray eels are coated in green goo. This stops them being harmed by the sharp rocks.

Going to ground
Stingrays swim around the seabed.

14

They swirl up clouds of sand so they can rest without being seen.

The flounder is a true **expert** in blending in. It can lie still as a statue.

Fish facts

The flounder can mimic its habitat in seconds.

Look out for
fish that trick!

expert to be good at something

habitat surroundings

mimic to look like

pursue to hunt

scout to look for

Index

beach 6

flounder 16, 18

frogfish 6, 7

habitat 4, 5, 18

moray eel 10, 13

reef 6, 10

rivers 2

seas 4

stingray 14

trout 4, 5

trumpetfish 9

Fish that fool

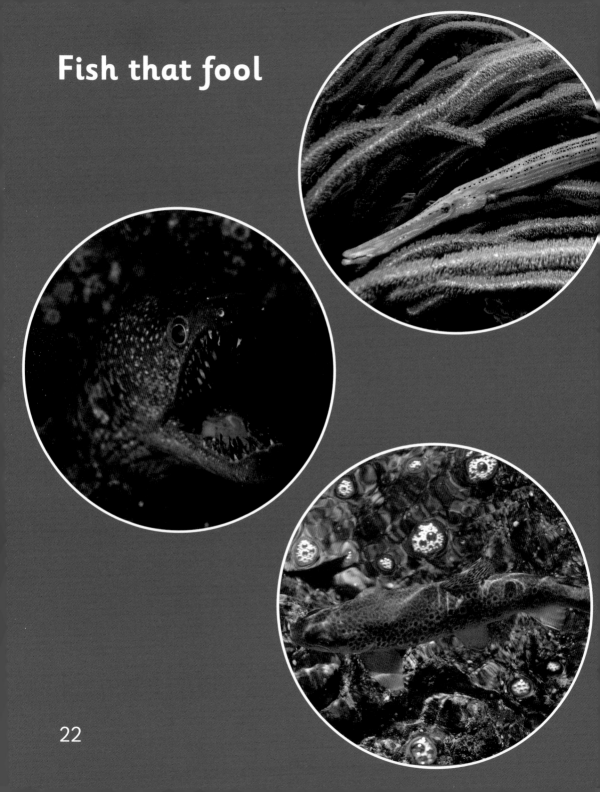

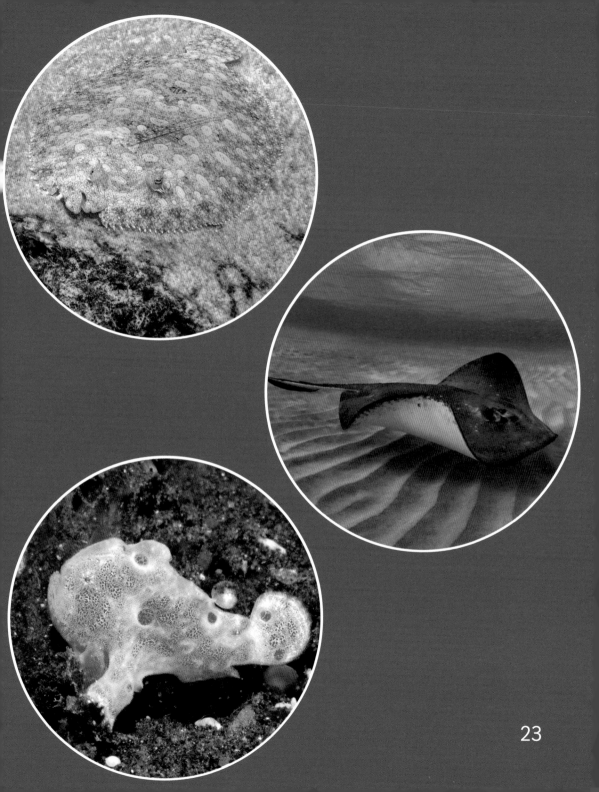

🐾 Review: After reading 🐾

Use your assessment from hearing the children read to choose any GPCs, words or tricky words that need additional practice.

Read 1: Decoding

- On page 4, point to the phrase **blends in**. Ask the children: What does this mean? Ensure they check the context of the sentence to understand the meaning. (e.g. *merges with; has the same colours as the creek*) Point out how "blends" in a cook book would mean something else, such as whisk, stir, mix.

- Ask the children to read these words. Can they point to the words with the /oo/ sound and the words with the /yoo/ sound?

  true   pursue   goo   statue   blue

- Challenge the children to take turns to read aloud a "Fish facts" box. Say: Can you blend in your head as you read the words?

Read 2: Prosody

- Model reading pages 10 and 11 to the children as if you were presenting a nature documentary.

- Point out how you paused at the ellipsis (for suspense), then speeded up for the action on page 11.

- Challenge the children to read the pages with expression to grab the listeners' attention!

Read 3: Comprehension

- Ask the children to describe any amazing fish they've seen in real life or on documentaries.

- Discuss the title with the children. Ask: What alternative title would work too? (e.g. *Clever Fish*; *Fish that Trick*; *Fishy Self-defence*) Ask the children to explain their choices.

- Focus on skimming and scanning skills.
  - Model looking for information about a specific fish, such as trout. Say: "Trout" isn't on the contents page so I'll scan for **trout**. Model scanning the pages then say: Let's check the index next, and model looking up pages 4 and 5.
  - Ask the children to skim the book to decide which chapter they think is the most interesting, and why.

- Turn to pages 22 and 23 and ask the children to talk about each picture, telling you what is special about each fish.